BUGS MAZES

Fran Newman-D'Amico

DOVER PUBLICATIONS, INC.
Mineola, New York

Bibliographical Note

Bugs Mazes is a new work, first published by Dover
Publications, Inc., in 2002.

International Standard Book Number
ISBN-13: 978-0-486-42173-5
ISBN-10: 0-486-42173-2

Manufactured in the United States by Courier Corporation
42173208
www.doverpublications.com

Note

In this little book you will find 48 mazes—puzzles with pictures of many types of bugs. Each bug is on its way somewhere, and you can help it get there as you draw a line from Start to Finish. You will help Bumblebee get to his hive, and show Butterfly the way to some lovely flowers, and much more. Try to finish all of the mazes before checking the Solutions, which begin on page 52. To have even more fun, you can color in the finished mazes with colored pencils or crayons. Enjoy!

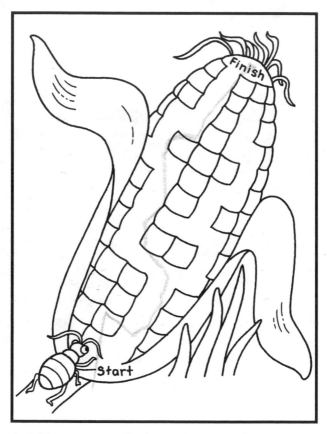

Aphid wants to climb to the top of the ear of corn. Show him the way to get there.

4

Little Moth is on her way to the tulips. Can you help her get to them?

Centipede wants to climb up the garden wall.
Show him the way to go.

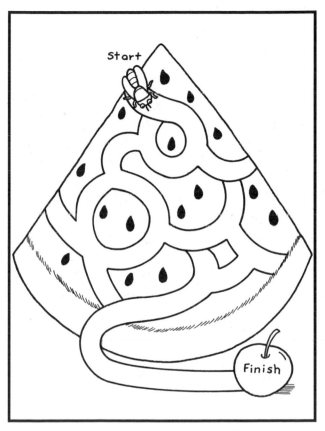

Tiny Midge loves to eat sweet fruit. Help her find her way through the watermelon to the cherry.

7

Stinkbug loves juicy tomatoes. Help him climb to the top of these plants.

Ground Beetle knows there is a piece of cake nearby. Show him the way across the table.

Lacewing can't wait to fly to the top of this tree.
Please show her how to get there.

10

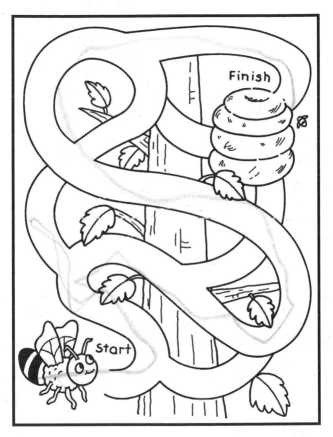

Where is Bumblebee's hive? Help him get to it!

Scorpion is meeting her brother at the cactus.
Find the path that will get her there.

12

Start

Finish

Grasshopper is on her way home to her patch of grass. Help her hop to it right away!

Start

Finish

There's another yummy leaf for Caterpillar to munch. Please show him the way to it.

14

Water Boatman is late! Help him make his way quickly to the sailboat!

15

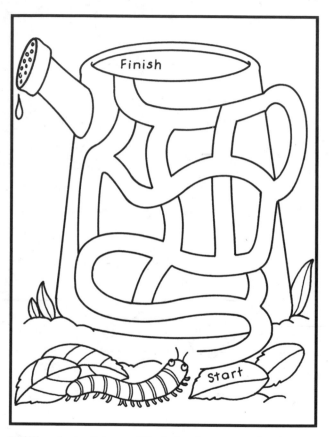

Millipede is thirsty. Find the best way for her to get to the top of the watering can.

16

Tired Termite is ready for a nap. Help him find his way back to his log.

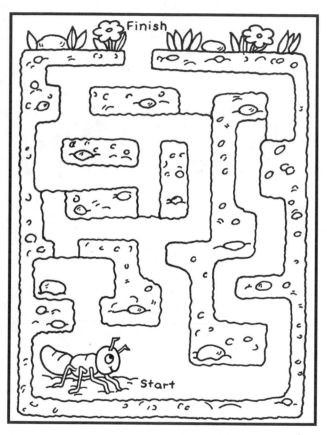

Ant wants to go out to play with her friends.
Show her the way through the tunnel.

18

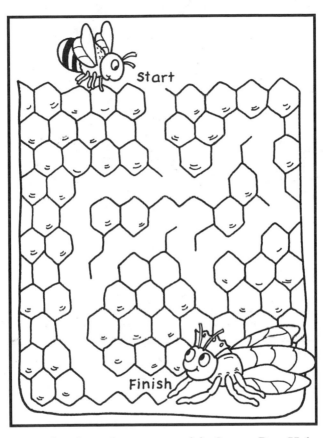

Honeybee is on her way to visit Queen Bee. Help Honeybee find a path through the honeycomb.

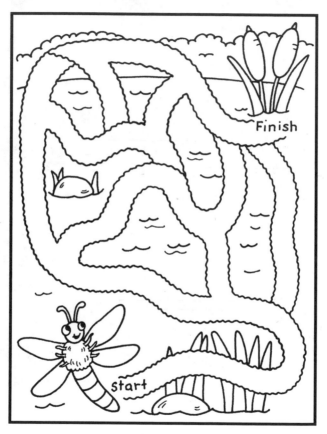

Doodlebug sees those bulrushes on the other side
of the water. Help him find the way to reach them.

20

Slug is ready to slither his way through the garden to get to the fence. Can you show him the way?

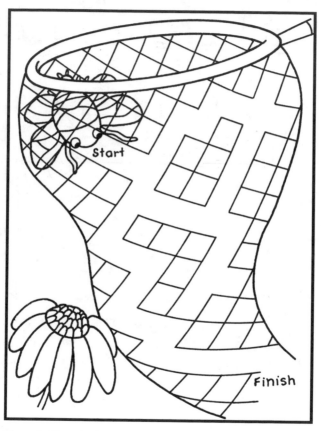

Start

Finish

Oops! Cicada is stuck in the net! Help her get to the bottom of the net and find a way out.

22

Butterfly has spotted some lovely flowers across the grass. Can you show her the way to them?

Start

Finish

Glowworm is ready to light the way to the log.
Find the path that will take him there.

24

Earthworm knows that there is a fat mushroom at the bottom of the tunnel. Can you help her get to it?

25

Roach is ready to race to the top of the soup can.
Show him the way to run!

Start

Finish

Dragonfly wants to visit Frog on his lily pad in the pond. Show her how to get there.

Mayfly thinks that he can reach the kite high in the sky. Can you find a way there?

Cricket is a long way from the forest. Help him cross the pond to get home.

Waterbug can't wait to swim with the friendly fish.
Help Waterbug find his way through the water.

30

Flea would like to jump onto that dog. Show Flea the way to get to it.

31

Slow-moving Snail can't wait to get out of the water. Help her find her way there.

Whirligig Beetle loves to spin around and around.
Help him find his way to the lily pad.

Can you help Inchworm "inch" her way up to the top of the garden hose to get a drop of water?

Locust loves to eat grapes! Help her nibble her way to the last grape in the bunch.

Walking Stick wants to wander up to the top branches of the tree. Won't you find him a path?

36

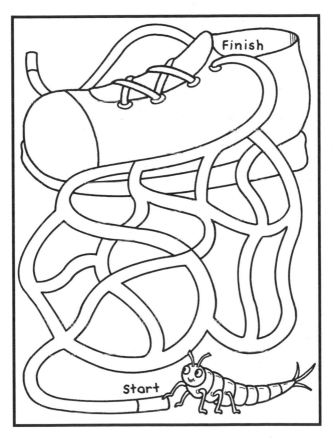

Silverfish is about to slither his way into the sneaker! Please show him how to get there.

37

Start

Finish

Wasp would love to smell that beautiful rose. Can you show him how to "buzz, buzz" his way to that flower?

38

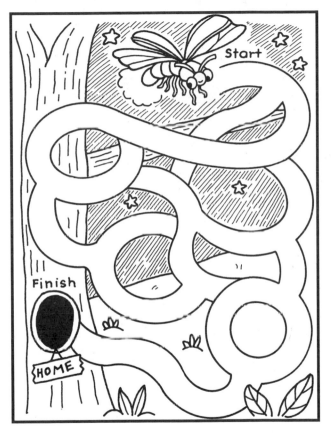

The stars are out, and Firefly is lighting up the dark. Please help her find her way back to her home in the tree. 39

Praying Mantis wants to sunbathe on that rock down below. Help him find his way there.

40

Spider wants to get to Fly, who is stuck in the middle of the web. What path should Spider take?

41

Bristleworm is on her way to see Crab and Lobster.
Find a path that will take her to both friends.

Can you help Ladybug pay a visit to Acorn and then find her way to the cherry at the end?

Housefly loves pears and apples. Help her fly to the pear, and then back around to the apple.

Like Housefly, Wasp loves to eat fruit. Help him find his way along the path to the juicy apple.

Shield Bug wants to get to her babies right away. Can you find a path for her to follow?

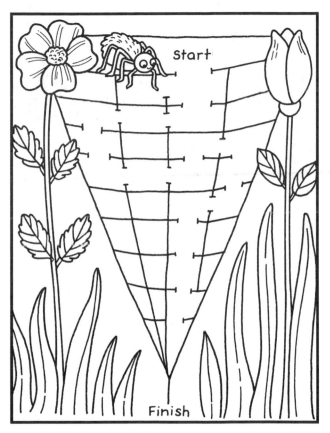

Start

Finish

Triangle Spider is at the top of his web. Find the
way for him to get to the bottom of the web.

Start

Finish

Here is Earwig at the top of the flowerpot. Please help her find a path to get to the bottom.

Little Larva loves to chew on tasty leaves. Show him how to get to the leaf at the top of this pear.

49

Pond Skater loves to "skate" her way across the water.
Show her a path to follow to get across the pond.

50

Hornet has been out for hours. Help him find a path that will take him back to the barn.

Solutions

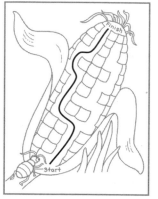

Page 4

Page 5

Page 6

Page 7

Page 8

Page 10

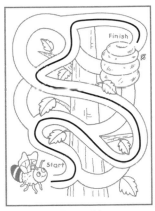

Page 11

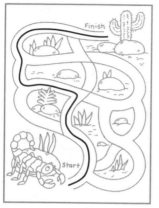

Page 12

Page 13

Page 14

Page 15

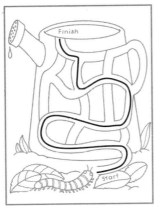

Page 16

Start
Finish

Page 17

Page 18

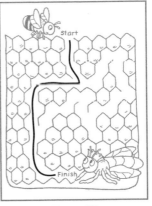

Page 19

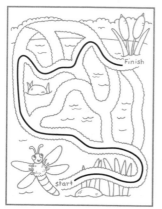

Page 20

Page 21

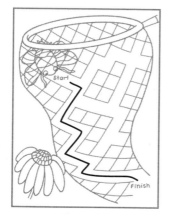

Page 22

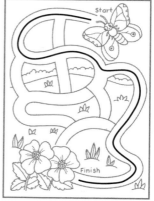

Page 23

Page 24

Page 25

Page 26

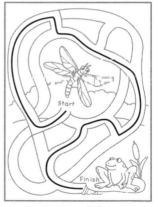

Page 27

Page 28

Page 29

Page 30

Page 31

Page 32

Page 33

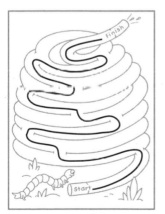

Page 34

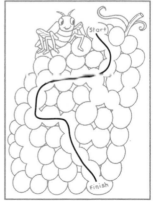

Page 35

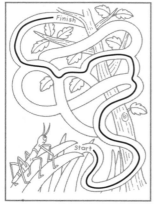

Page 36

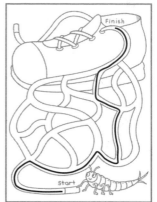

Page 37

Page 38

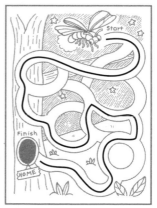

Page 39

Page 40

Page 41

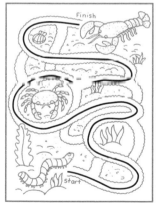

Page 42

Page 43

Page 44

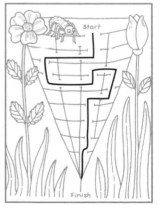

Page 45

Page 46

Page 47

Page 48

Page 49

Page 50

Page 51